Fears and Phobias

MARGARET O. HYDE

McGRAW-HILL BOOK COMPANY

New York • St. Louis • San Francisco
Auckland • Bogotá • Düsseldorf
Johannesburg • London • Madrid
Mexico • Montreal • New Delhi
Panama • Paris • São Paulo
Singapore • Sydney • Tokyo
Toronto

Library of Congress Cataloging in Publication Data

Hyde, Margaret Oldroyd, date.
   Fears and phobias.

    Bibliography: p.
    Includes index.
    1. Fear—Juvenile literature. 2. Phobias—
Juvenile literature.   I. Title.
BF575.F2H93   152.4   77-78757
ISBN 0-07-031648-1 lib. bdg.

   2345MUBP7898

For Holly L. Pattin
and Karen A. Pattin

CONTENTS

FEARS AND PHOBIAS

chapter 1

LIVING WITH FEAR

Someone shouts *"Fire!"* in a theater, and fear spreads through the auditorium. People rush toward the exits, and the crush of the crowd is so great that no one can get through a doorway. Bodies are jammed together in a panic that need not have been. Intelligent leadership could have kept the crowd's fear under control and prevented many deaths.

The fear that comes with disaster may serve an important purpose in alerting you to danger. If a car comes toward you, the physiological changes produced by fear give you the extra energy needed to run out of its path. The person who claims to be fearless ignores a healthy feeling in the case of actual threat. But fear may get out of control, causing panic or even paralysis. For example, most individuals will heed warnings to move to a higher place when a river is overflowing its banks; but some will stay in their homes and drown as they cling in terror to the things they know.

Are you unusual because you fear the dark? Certainly you are not alone, but whether or not your fear is realistic depends on the circumstances. Walking through a large city park at night in fear of muggers is different from the fear of walking past a cemetery on a dark country road. In both cases, however, the fear may be very real.

A phobia is a real fear, but it is a reaction that is out of proportion to a specific situation or thing. Phobias cannot be voluntarily controlled, and they lead to total avoidance of the feared situations. One classic case of phobia concerns Professor William Ellery Leonard, who was terrified by a locomotive when he was a child. This had such far-reaching effects that his phobia virtually kept him a prisoner in the university town where he taught. Professor Leonard described seizures that terrified him. When his anxiety attacks occurred, he had to retreat to what he felt was a safe place. For those who suffer phobias today, there are many new methods of treatment that can help them to overcome their severe, irrational fears.

Anxiety is a form of fear that may interfere with the quality of one's life from a limited to a large degree. Even when the cause is ill-defined, anxiety may pervade much of everyday activity. Fortunately, with proper treatment, most people can control this form of fear.

Some people purposely put themselves in dangerous situations because they enjoy the feeling of risk. The athlete who pits ability against a powerful obstacle finds pleasure in the challenge. For example, a skier who conquers a difficult slope may have been frightened during the run, but in the end s/he achieves a great sense of accomplishment from overcoming the element of fear.

You may consciously look for fearful situations where you can identify with the adventure or disaster. Scary as they may be, horror and suspense movies, detective and mystery stories, and scary amusement park rides are enjoyed by many people. They all arouse basic survival instincts. When the enemy is defeated or the threat removed, there is a pleasant sense of relief.

Almost everyone knows the look and sound of fear. Suppose a cry pierces the distant air. You can tell from the sound that someone is frightened even though you have no idea what is causing the fear. You can picture the distorted face of the person. The eyes are open, and the muscles of the lower eyelids are tense. The upper eyelids are raised, and so are the eyebrows. Eyebrows appear to be straightened, and there are horizontal wrinkles across the forehead. This is the physical face of fear.

But fear wears many masks. From the unconscious anxieties to the obvious fears of panic, there is much to explore. There is much to find out about how to control your fears rather than be victimized by them. Let's begin by examining fear in a relatively quiet place such as a field or a meadow. Fear is there, as everywhere.

chapter 2

THE CLIMATE OF FEAR IN A QUIET FIELD

Suppose you are sitting in a quiet meadow late in the afternoon. The sunset casts a glow of orange light through the trees at the edge of the meadow, and all is peaceful. You are resting quietly when you hear something rustle, and a small snake appears in the grass near your feet. Suddenly there is a climate of fear. Your body responds by increasing the flow of adrenalin, a hormone that is secreted by a pair of glands that lie above your kidneys. Your heart rate increases, your hands feel cold, and perspiration dampens your palms. Increased amounts of blood are sent to your brain and muscles, mobilizing your body for fight or flight. All of this happens without any effort on your part. Your unconscious reactions have prepared you for action, but the snake slithers away and once more you relax in the meadow. You may tell yourself that the snake was not poisonous anyway and was probably more afraid of you than you were of it. But the next time you see a snake you will most likely experience the same fear and bodily changes.

You are probably not the only one to experience fear in the meadow. Other animals respond to the environment with different senses and may experience varying amounts of fear because of your presence. The ant which crawls nearby lives in a very limited world and does not see you as it follows the track from its anthill to a source of food. The ant puts its nose to the ground, smelling its way with no fear that you might step on it and extinguish its existence. But if you crush some other ants, it will exhibit some apparent signs of fear. No one really knows if the ant you have been watching is frightened by the crushed members of its own species, but it will appear to be frantic. This reaction may be due to the odor of the damaged ants. You, of course, will have no fear of the harmless, little ant crawling through the grass beside you.

The frog croaking in the nearby pond doesn't see you either. Although the frog's field of vision is wide, it does not see very clearly. It is conscious only of fast-moving objects, such as the flies on which it feeds. But if you make a sudden move toward the frog, it will see a large body, assume you are an enemy, and be frightened enough to jump into the water to escape you. You probably will be amused rather than frightened.

Now suppose a rattlesnake is resting near the frog. What happens when it approaches the frog? The frog doesn't move. You might assume that the frog remains motionless because it is afraid of the snake, but that is not true. Actually, the frog does not move because it cannot see the small body slithering slowly in its direction. The frog's vision is limited to the kind it needs for catching insects.

What about the rattlesnake and you? The snake has a sense detector that is sensitive to heat and can warn the snake of danger when there is a temperature change of as little as 1/1,000th of a degree centigrade. The rattlesnake may sense your presence by this detector and prepare to attack. At the same time, you will be frightened by the rattlesnake because your eyes have detected it. But as the snake moves away from you, your sense of fear will gradually decrease.

A bird flies overhead. The bird does not frighten you, for it is no threat to your well-being and you actually enjoy watching it circle above looking for food on the ground. The bird's vision is good, so good that it can watch a mouse from high in the sky. Suddenly, the bird swoops down to catch the mouse on the ground close to you, and for a moment you experience a pang of fear. But as the bird captures its prey and returns to the air, your fear disappears.

Bees fly near you as you rest in the meadow. Even though they are small, you are mildly frightened because you know that they can sting you. But the bees do not see you as they fly straight ahead to gather nectar and pollen from the flowers of the meadow. Bees have eyes which see in a very special way. Their eyes are developed to see bright patterns of flowers in full bloom, the source of their nectar. Of course, if a bee happens to land on you and you injure it by brushing it or crushing part of it, the bee may sting in an effort to protect itself. People who are allergic to bee stings have good reason for the intense fear they experience when they hear the buzzing of a bee.

Plants that are familiar because of their poison may arouse fear in a person resting in a meadow. If you roll over and discover you are lying in poison ivy, you may feel apprehensive because you know it can cause intense skin irritation. Nettles are another variety of plant which grow in meadows and cause pain to humans. A nettle bears a number of hairs and bristles which contain an irritating fluid. If you have walked or rolled in an area where these plants grow, you may be mildly frightened. The jagged splintery needles that are formed when the tip of a stinging nettle hair is broken penetrates human skin and leaves a sting that may last only half an hour but may cause severe burning and itching during that time. Although one does not usually panic at the sight of nettle plants, anyone familiar with them may feel a few pangs of fear when falling in their direction.

When the sky grows dark above the meadow, certain noises may frighten you. Nighthawks climb high in the sky above you, beating their long wings. As they come back toward earth, their eerie cries pierce the air at regular intervals.

More frightening to most people is the sight of a bat which may dart from the edge of the meadow and sweep toward the grass in search of gnats and moths. Many people have heard that bats can steer away from obstacles (such as people) in their paths, but you may still find bats frightening. If such is the case, the climate of fear is confined to your own body, for the bat is unaware of your presence. It is sending out signals somewhat like the clicking noise which you can make with your tongue, but you do not hear the signals because they are so high-pitched that no human can hear them. This special radar system helps the bat locate its prey. Adjusting its position to that of the insect it has detected, the bat snaps up the insect and continues its search for food. After the bat flies away, your body quickly readjusts to a situation of peaceful rest.

Consider the things that might trigger your fear in a meadow, or in any other place for that matter. In every case, they are creatures, plants, objects, or experiences which have some potential to harm you or which you think will harm you. One definition of fear is *a reaction to a recognized threat which is characterized by an impulse to escape danger and a feeling of disagreeable tension.*

The intensity of fear in any situation varies among individuals and depends partly on the potential danger which causes the fear. While fears in the meadow, in the city, or in any other place might range from very mild fright to panic, there is no exact way to measure them except in the laboratory. But it is clear that to some degree humans, dogs, cats, and many other animals all experience the natural reactions of fight or flight in various stressful situations.

chapter 3
CHILDREN'S FEARS

The fears of very young children come and go. One day two-year-old David will scream when he hears the noise of a vacuum cleaner. He is terrified now, but yesterday he paid no attention to it. He heard no other loud noises yesterday or today which might have caused this new fear. But David's fear of the vacuum cleaner is a common one at age two, and it will probably disappear as suddenly as it arose.

Certain fears are quite common in young children, and they appear at various ages as a child learns and matures. By studying what frightens the very young, learning how they react to fear, how their fears change, and how some fears produce problems in later years, experts are helping both young and old.

Can you remember some of the things that frightened you when you were very young? Fear researchers use a technique of questioning people about their early fears with some degree of success, but most of the things which frighten young children are quickly forgotten.

A woman named Lucy had a different experience, however. She was unable to discard one of her childhood fears. In fact, Lucy's fear of automobiles was so unusual that she consulted a therapist, Dr. Charles Odier. In his book, *Patterns of Magical Thinking*, he describes her case. It was through a dream that Lucy recalled the origin of her fear. She dreamed that a baby in a carriage was run over by a large automobile. She told the doctor that she recognized herself as the baby in the dream. After this, Lucy was able to recall a terrifying experience from her early childhood in which she was paralyzed with fear while playing in the garden near a garage. As a young child, she had imagined the garage to be a big cage. When a car came out of it, she associated the noise of the motor with the loud roar of an animal coming to get her. Although in later years she forgot the experience, she continued to suffer from an intense fear of cars. Lucy's fear of automobiles occurred only when she was outside a car. Then she would automatically say, "Be careful, here comes a crusher!" To her, all drivers were "crushers," who were out to kill pedestrians. Riding inside a car, however, Lucy was not abnormally fearful. The entire case was extremely complex, but what is of interest here is the fact that Lucy's phobia had its roots in her childhood when she imagined the car to be an animal that was out to harm her. Her acute feeling of helplessness as a young child grew into such anxiety that all cars appeared dangerous to her unless she was riding safely within. But relatively few children experience fears which are so traumatic that they develop into phobias.

Every healthy child experiences fears. Newborn babies react to intense, unexpected noises. This reaction, which doctors refer to as the startle response, is present at birth and may be an inborn response which later becomes a fear response. Although fear is difficult to examine in the very young because an infant's expressions are difficult to interpret, some studies have yielded interesting results. The fear of an approaching object appears to be present early in life. Some infants as young as two weeks seemed frightened when an object was moved toward them at close range. In one study of over forty infants made by T. G. R. Bower and others* in 1970, an apparent fear reaction was reported

*Bower, T. G. R., J. M. Broughton and M. K. Moore. "Infant Responses to Approaching Objects," *Percept, Psychophysics,*1970, pp. 193–6.

when a small, soft rubber cube was moved to within eight inches of a baby's face. Each time this was done, the infant cried loudly, put its hands between its face and the object, and pulled away from it. There was no response when the object was moved *away* from the baby.

Great Aunt Tillie might be less displeased with baby's shrieks when she moves close to express love if she realized that babies are instinctively frightened by the approach of a stranger. Perhaps the approach of a distant relative or any other person strange to the baby results in fear because of this reaction or so-called looming response.

Fear of strangers appears to be almost universal in infants in the second half of the first year of life. While 98 percent of a sample group of infants between the ages of two and six months will smile in response to the face of any individual, indiscriminate smiling usually ceases after that age. Dr. Marshall Klaus of Case Western Reserve University in Cleveland, Ohio, has studied the facial bonding between mother and child, which he believed occurs during the first few hours of life. This is the first evidence of social interaction in humans and is believed to form the basis for further social learning.

Once babies can distinguish faces (at about six months), they react to strangers with fear. This fear usually continues until the first birthday and sometimes through the second year of life. The fear response is a further stage in social interaction.

The fear behavior of one-year-olds usually varies according to the nearness of the mother or father. For example, in one experiment there was less evidence of fear in a stressful situation when a baby was in the mother's lap than when the mother moved four feet away from the child. Another factor which influences the fear reaction at this age is the stranger's behavior. When the baby was not touched and the stranger smiled and played peek-a-boo, there were some positive reactions from one-year-olds.

Fear of strangers is considered just one aspect of the fear of new situations or things. Studies of thousands of normal children have shown that many fears do come and go in a somewhat ordered pattern. Although each child exhibits some individual variations, most two-year-olds are afraid of loud noises, and few children seem to fear the dark before the age of two or three. At two and a half, children generally fear moving objects, such as large trucks, and people who appear unexpectedly from a place such as a door not commonly used.

Fear of animals is common to most children and seems to begin at the age of three. Five-year-olds are less afraid of animals in general, but they are more apprehensive of being bitten by a dog. They are also afraid of bodily harm, of falling, and of mother's not returning when she goes out at night.

Fear of the dark continues for a number of years but usually lessens by the time a child is eight or nine. Fear of ghosts and witches, haunted houses, or other supernatural phenomena continues for several years. Of course, some people never outgrow these and other fears. A great many young children who read about lions, tigers, and dinosaurs, as well as the supernatural, seek reassurance from their parents that these fierce beasts are not in the backyard or immediate environment. One of the major sources of trust in authority comes from the relief from anxiety that a young child experiences on being told that there are *no* lions and *no* dinosaurs anywhere nearby.

While ten-year-olds are not especially fearful, wild animals and snakes are commonly feared at this age. As the child's horizons broaden, fears that are not so personal are introduced. Television, books, and radio may stimulate other fears.

While each age has its characteristic fears, most pass harmlessly. It helps when people realize that fear is not shameful and that it is natural for a child to withdraw from those things which seem harmful. This is typical of survival patterns in young and old and in other animals as well as humans. For example, fear of heights is common to many animals as well as to the very young child.

Psychologist Eleanor Gibson was picnicking one day on the rim of the Grand Canyon when she wondered whether or not a young baby would recognize the danger at the brink or would fall off into space. Her speculations led to some famous experiments which are known as the visual cliff experiments. An arrangement of simulated levels was used. The effect of a one-foot drop was created by placing a piece of heavy glass some twelve inches above a piece of patterned material. A board at the same level as the glass was covered with the same patterned material. On the side opposite the simulated drop, or "cliff" side, was another sheet of glass with the patterned material immediately beneath it, giving the appearance of a shallow drop.

The visual cliff. Redrawn from Sight and Mind *by Lloyd Kaufman, Oxford University Press, 1974.*

For the experiments, young children were placed on the board while their mothers called from the cliff side. In general, children peered down at the glass and backed away from what looked like the steep side—even after they'd touched the glass. Babies as young as six months discerned that the patterned material seemed far beneath them and were afraid of falling off. Of thirty-six infants tested over a period of time, only three crept off the "brink" onto the glass suspended a foot above the pattern.

Chickens less than twenty-four hours old were tested on the visual cliff, and they, too, avoided the deep area. Young goats and lambs were tested as soon as they could stand, and no goat or lamb ever stepped off the deep side. Kittens "froze" or crawled backward when placed on the glass over the deep side.

From these and numerous other experiments, it seems clear that in many species of animals fear or perception of height appears very early. Even infants who have never experienced the sensation of falling seem to fear falling off a cliff.

Loss of support and sudden loud noises also cause fear responses in most young infants, as well as in animals of other species. Despite this and other common fear responses, however, experimenters such as Alexander Thomas, Stella Chess, and Herbert G. Birch report that children do show distinct individuality in temperament in the first weeks of life. (This difference is independent of the treatment they receive and of their parents' personalities.) Thomas et al. studied the response of an infant to a new object or person in order to see whether the child would accept the new experience or withdraw from it. In most cases, a child's original reaction seemed to be retained over the years, although temperaments can and do change.

Consider the case of Grace. From the start, she probably cried loudly when someone slammed a door in the hospital nursery even though other babies continued to sleep. Throughout infancy Grace had withdrawal reactions whenever she faced a new situation, such as entering kindergarten, or encountered a new challenge. But these withdrawal reactions were soon forgotten because Grace always adjusted well once the newness wore off. Grace had many friends and few problems until the fifth grade, when she had to transfer to a new and larger school. The move caused her great fear and worry. These emotions puzzled her parents until her history was reviewed and it was recognized that she had a fundamental tendency to withdraw from new situations and to adapt to them slowly. Understanding of a person's temperament can help in dealing with a wide variety of situations.

One of the most pervasive fears in the lives of boys concerns contact sports. Many boys and young men are under great social pressure to participate in sandlot and school teams because of the widespread national interest in hockey, football, and other rough sports. Some psychologists believe this causes great anxiety in many of these young people who do not like to admit their fear of getting hurt while participating in contact sports. Some even develop a school phobia because coaches, headmasters, and parents demand that everyone engage in physically bruising sports activities. In today's world, there is more chance for a young man to have an appropriate male role identity based on factors other than *machismo.* In large numbers of schools and families, however, physical strength is still equated with manliness.

There are many theories to explain why people develop their own special personalities. A human personality is a total pattern of typical ways of behaving and thinking that makes up the individual's unique and distinctive method of adjusting to his or her environment. Obviously, many factors are involved. One of these factors appears to be the physiological structure of the body. Both heredity and environment appear to determine the role of fear as a person develops, but fear is hard to examine, especially in the young. In the *Origins of Fear,** which examines the expression and development of fear in human infants in various settings, the authors question which responses of an infant or young child would qualify as fear. Many experts agree that it is difficult to even define fear. No matter what the temperament of the infant, many fears are learned. Only a small percentage of ten-

*Lewis, Michael, and Leonard Rosenbaum, eds. *The Origins of Fear*, New York: John Wiley and Sons, 1974.

month-olds reacted with fear when they saw a doctor preparing an injection like one given to them just a few weeks earlier. These few had already learned to fear the pain which they remembered. After eleven and twelve months of age, however, most infants fearfully withdrew from the anticipated painful injection. This kind of fear is obviously learned at a very early age.

Most one-year-olds have learned to turn to mother or father when there is a frightening or uncertain situation, but at six months this form of security has not been learned. Between the ages of five and eighteen months children are frightened by the approach of a mechanical dog or by the popping of a jack-in-the-box, but few older children are afraid of these toys.

Fire is a continued source of fear for many children, and the fear of fire is indeed a healthy and protective one. It is most common at the age of six. When it does not disappear naturally, parents can help relieve it by letting the child assist at family barbecues where fire is under control. Watching adults burn trash where such fires are permitted, helping to light candles at the dinner table, and sharing in the enjoyment of a fire in a fireplace may also help relieve excessive fear of fire.

Although children back away from things they

fear, there is often a second stage in overcoming a fear in which they approach the feared object too closely. Many who were very afraid of fires go through a stage of actually setting them before settling into a stage where they respect fire and its constructive use when under control.

If you have a brother or sister in the pre-school group or have contact with other young children, you may find the following suggestions useful:

Respect children's fears and realize that they will outgrow most of them. Telling children that only babies are afraid, or making fun of their fears, does not help the situation. When children withdraw from fearful situations, permit a reasonable time for this reaction to subside before attempting to help with adjustment. Listen to their descriptions of what seems to be frightening and reassure them if there is no real reason for the fears. Discuss fears frankly and admit to real threats.

Help children to grow familiar with fearful situations a little at a time. Getting acquainted with a puppy or small dog may help make a large dog seem less frightening. Looking down from a small elevation, then increasing height gradually, may help children who are afraid of heights. This procedure may be used in hilly parks or with big boxes.

Realize that it is normal for children to have some fears, and do not force them to try to overcome fears until they seem ready to do so. Forcing a young child into a lake, ocean, or other large body of water may lengthen the time of learning to swim.

Certainly, there are many kinds of fear and theories about fear in young children. Two interesting conclusions follow. First, experiments seem to show that when a situation that arouses a low intensity of fear is paired with another low intensity situation, intense fear may result. For example, the appearance of a large dog combined with the roar of thunder may cause fear greater than the sum of the two. Second, the presence or absence of a mother or other trusted person greatly influences the degree of fear with which the child responds. If a mother goes to the hospital for an emergency operation, a child may have nightmares and small fears may become big ones. On the other hand, a situation which might be very frightening to a child alone (such as being lost in the woods) does not arouse much fear if a parent is present.

How one learns to cope with fears during early childhood may play a very important part in how one copes with fears of many varieties in later life.

chapter 4

FEAR IN PETS AND EXPERIMENTAL ANIMALS

Fear reactions in cats, dogs, lions, gorillas, people, and other animals differ from species to species and from individual to individual. There is much overlap in the things which arouse fear in humans and those which arouse fear in other species, and certain situations appear generally to be more feared than others. Learning about the fears of various kinds of animals has helped individuals to understand and cope with their own fears and helped therapists in their work with people. It has even played a part in the way some veterinarians care for pets.

How can fear in animals be recognized? In addition to the obvious reactions of fight or flight, some responses are similar to the ones exhibited by frightened people. These include "freezing," curling up, taking cover, seeking the company of others, and calling for help. Many humans recognize the alarm calls of birds and mammals by their very tone. Various species of birds and mammals use the alarm calls of another species as warnings to escape danger. A wide variety of animals respond to potential danger cues through their senses of smell, sight, and/or hearing.

Fear responses to a sudden approach or strangeness are common. The fear of strangeness has an interesting aspect in the case of imprinting, which occurs with certain animals, especially birds that live on the ground and mammals that live in flocks. The term *imprinting* can be defined as the learning of parental characteristics by young animals. Imprinting takes place during a very brief period of time early in the life of the animal.

Pet geese are often the subject of experiments which show how animals learn to recognize the security of parents and to fear other animals. Professor Konrad Lorenz, a famous Viennese naturalist, used the eggs of the graylag goose in a popular experiment to demonstrate imprinting. After the eggs hatched, he discovered that the goslings would become attached to any large moving object, including himself, if they were separated from their mother during the imprinting period. They would follow Professor Lorenz in a long line across the fields, much as they would have followed their real mother.

Very young chicks will follow a person who clucks and walks away, and many other animals show this kind of socialization. Normally, the young become agitated and frightened when they are separated from the mother or mother object. This and other facts have led scientists to believe that imprinting reduces anxiety.

Pet dogs show signs of imprinting in the form of attachment to the dogs or people to whom they are exposed during the third to seventh week after birth. All new puppies that become pets experience socialization. Have you ever watched a puppy getting acquainted in its new home? If a puppy was born in a kennel and very few people touched it, talked to it, or spent time nearby for the first five weeks of its life, the puppy may be afraid of the people who take it home even though they are kind to it. But after a few weeks of gentle handling, fear reactions disappear. If puppies are handled by people at three or four weeks of age, most dogs show no fear reactions by the time they are five weeks old.

Suppose a litter of puppies is allowed to run wild without any attention from people for a period of twelve weeks. Such puppies will be very timid when near humans and almost impossible to handle. They may need some hand-feeding and much loving care to overcome their fear of people. Keeping them in a confined area helps, but scientists who study animal behavior believe that dogs who have no contact with humans during the first twelve weeks of their lives will always be somewhat timid around human beings and will be less responsive as pets than those handled by people from birth.

Pets are frequently selected for the reputation of the breed's disposition. For example, basset hounds, spaniels, poodles, and dachshunds are known for their mild temperaments. And some may have characteristics which make them unsuitable for families with young children. But there are variations of fear responses even in dogs of the same breed.

Dogs and humans share many traits, and one of these is fear. In 1960, scientists at the Neuropsychiatric Laboratory of North Little Rock Veterans Administration Hospital in Arkansas began breeding two different strains of purebred pointers in an effort to study their behavior. They bred one line of pointers which developed abnormal behavior of a "neurotic" type and one line which was stable. Dr. Oddist D. Murphee and his colleagues explored the behavior of these different strains of pointers over a period of years, using a wide variety of tests. Nothing was done to aggravate or increase the timidity of the nervous strain of dogs. They were studied in relation to the stable strain to try to learn more about environmental and hereditary differences.

The behavior of the nervous strain was characterized by excessive timidity, extreme startle response, reduced activity in exploring surroundings, and marked avoidance of humans as well as frequent immobility in their presence. Some nervous dogs actually became rigid with fear in the presence of humans; if a person pushed the dogs's head down, its back feet would actually spring up.

Psychologists, psychiatrists, biochemists, and veterinarians are still studying fear in the pointers described above, as these animals are used for psychiatric research. While dogs are not true models for human behavior disorders, there *are* many common characteristics. For example, some of the mind-body related, or psychosomatic illnesses suffered by humans are also present in dogs. And the symptoms of rigid posture found in some emotionally disturbed people are also seen in some dogs. It is hoped that experimenting with fear reactions and other behavior in these dogs will lead to significant advances in the field of human psychiatry.

Another approach to the study of fear in animals is demonstrated by the work of Dr. F.

Brunner, a doctor at the Veterinary Hospital in Vienna, Austria. Dr. Brunner works with dogs and cats that have behavioral disorders which cause problems for their owners as well as for the pets themselves. He does not believe that there is enough knowledge at present to determine whether certain fears and other behavior problems are caused by the animal's environment or heredity. Many individual behavior variations become serious problems, however. Treatment or therapy by a professional trainer can often change the situation and, in some cases, actually save the life of the pet.

Take the case of Chauncey, an overly fearful sheep dog which would jump on his master's bed during thunderstorms. The fright response first occurred at the age of three years after the dog was left alone in the house during a violent storm. Corrective training through a method known as conditioning helped Chauncey to overcome his abnormal fear of thunderstorms. The therapist-trainer could not explain to the dog that thunder was harmless, but noises similar to those made by thunder were simulated at the clinic and followed by the gentle, reassuring voice of the trainer. When the dog, who had jumped on the bed, became calm, the trainer led him off the bed with a leash and praised him for getting off the bed. After each thunderclap, the procedure was repeated. Petting him, praising him, and staying close to him helped reassure Chauncey that nothing would harm him when there was a loud noise. This procedure helped to reduce the dog's fear of thunder.

Field observers of monkeys and apes report similar fears in these animals. P. Jay, a scientist who studied the behavior of a type of monkey in India, reported that forest groups gradually became accustomed to her presence so that she could follow them at a distance of about fifty feet. But when the monkeys were startled by any sudden noise or movement in the brush, they immediately fled from sight.

Fleeing is one major kind of fear response; seeking physical contact with companions is another. Anthropologist Jane van Lawick-Goodall carried out a long-term study of chimpanzees in Tanzania and included much information about fear responses in her detailed reports. One interesting observation concerned the hugging she witnessed between both young and old chimpanzees when they were frightened.

Many fears which people experience and many ways of handling these fears are better understood because of animal observation and experimentation. Fear of snakes is common among some birds, monkeys, apes, and humans, but whether this fear is learned or inborn is still a matter of dispute among experts. Certainly, fear of snakes is very intense in old world monkeys and apes.

When snakes were released in the monkey house of the London Zoo many years ago, the monkeys fled and screamed. But lemurs crowded to the front of the cages to watch the snakes. Lemurs are small, nocturnal animals that have large eyes, soft fur, and long tails. They belong to the family of primates, which includes monkeys, apes, and man, and their natural habitat is Madagascar and adjacent islands. This area is one of the few parts of the world where there are no poisonous snakes. At first glance, the difference in fear response between the lemurs and the monkeys might appear to be proof that fear of snakes is inborn protection developed through evolution. But it also might be interpreted to be the result of the handing down of a learned fear from one generation to the next. Many animal behaviorists have shown that some wild species pass on a learned fear from one generation to the next. Humans are not alone in cultural traditions that teach survival techniques.

According to some theories, the fear of snakes may be due to fear of certain types of movement.

But wild chimpanzees have shown fear of snakes whether they were moving quickly or sleeping quietly. And chimpanzees who are raised in zoos do not always show fear when confronted with a snake.

While many humans are mildly squeamish in the presence of snakes, only 20 percent of the students who were tested in one study expressed intense fear of them. Of this group, only 1–2 percent actually avoided snakes when in their presence.

While fear is an inborn emotional response in higher animals, only certain situations seem to evoke fear on cue. For example, humans may be genetically biased to respond to writhing motions with fear, since these motions represent a clue to danger. In humans, the form and intensity of fears vary with maturation. Because most adults have learned so many new behaviors, traces of early fears are obscured; but these early fears may have an unconscious influence on the development of anxieties and phobias later in their lives.

chapter 5
PHOBIAS

Sally is a fifteen-year-old girl who will not go on the class picnic because of her intense fear of being stung by a bee. She will not visit friends who live in the suburbs of the city or walk near any area where she might see a bee. Because her family wants to move to the country, Sally's fear of bees is creating a serious problem. Sally is not allergic to bees, and some members of her family feel that she is just trying to get special attention and stay in the city where she prefers to live. But Sally's fear is actually very real. She turns white when a bee comes near her, perspires, trembles, and feels dizzy. Sally is suffering from a phobia.

If Sally's family knew how to recognize a phobia, they would realize that she has no control over the excessive fear reaction she experiences in the presence of a bee. Even imagining that a bee is buzzing nearby causes intense physical and psychological fear in Sally. The muscular tension, fast breathing, perspiration, dryness of her mouth, weakness in her legs, and other symptoms are all involuntary, and Sally really does experience a feeling of panic far beyond that of reason. No one in her family can help her to understand that although a bee sting would hurt, it would not be serious. However, Sally can probably be helped to overcome her phobia if she is willing to go to a therapist for professional help.

Do you know someone who has a phobia? Many people express fears of certain kinds of animals, of flying in planes, or of being in the dark, in high places, or in crowds. The yardstick which is used to differentiate between so-called normal fears and phobias contains several tests for measurement. First, is the reaction inappropriate? Fear of a knife pointed at you is an appropriate or realistic fear, while fear of a knife on display on a store counter is not. Second, is there excessive preoccupation with the situation or object that is feared? If you are frightened one night while camping in the dark, this fear is not a phobia; but if you are intensely frightened whenever you are in the dark and this fear of the dark continues over a long period of time, you may be suffering from nyctophobia. The third measure on the yardstick is whether or not the fear is very intense. You may dislike the sight of a spider crawling nearby, or even feel that you are afraid of spiders, but unless you have a very intense fear of them you probably are not suffering from a phobia. Many people use the word *phobia* loosely to describe their dislike of crowds or of being in confined spaces, but unless the fear meets these tests, it is probably not a phobia.

People often say, "I suffer from claustrophobia," or "I'm acrophobic." Investigation frequently shows that these people are naming a phobia that is not only absent from their lives but one whose meaning they have confused. The following list of phobias is provided for those who would like to sort out the names of phobias and the objects or situations to which they refer.

acrophobia	height
agoraphobia	open spaces, market place, etc.
ailurophobia	cats
anthropophobia	people
aquaphobia	water
arachnophobia	spiders
astraphobia	lightning
brontophobia	thunder
claustrophobia	closed spaces
cynophobia	dogs
dementophobia	madness
equinophobia	horses

herptophobia	snakes, lizards, and other crawling things
mikrophobia	germs
murophobia	mice
mysophobia	germs, dirt
nyctophobia	darkness
pyrophobia	fire
thanatophobia	death
xenophobia	strangers
zoophobia	animals

This list is far from complete, and professionals recognize about five times as many phobias as are mentioned here. Some phobias have more than one name. For example, fear of thunder (brontophobia) is also known as keraunosphobia.

Psychologists and psychiatrists are more interested in the causes and cures of phobias than in the particular varieties from which people suffer, especially if a phobia creates a major problem in the lifestyle of a person. Some phobias are confined to infrequent occasions, while others pervade every waking minute of a person's life.

Consider the case of Cary, who suffers from agoraphobia. When Cary was about thirty years old she began feeling strange whenever she went shopping or walked along a street. Because she was uncomfortable about being in public places, she stayed home most of the time unless her husband went with her. When she tried going to the store alone, she experienced a feeling that something dreadful was going to happen to her. She grew breathless, had palpitations of the heart, and had to lean against a wall. The manager of the store called her husband at his office, and he came to take her home.

Fear of walking any distance alone is one of the symptoms of agoraphobics, and the panic which seized Cary in the store prevented her from having to walk the distance from the store to her home. Cary adjusted to her problem by confining her activities to her own home, but this restricted life was hardly a fulfilling one. Treatment might have relieved her symptoms and improved the quality of life for her and her family.

Some phobias cover such a wide range of fears that they are referred to as a phobic anxiety state. Dr. Isaac M. Marks, a psychiatrist who practiced at Maudsley Hospital in London, England, describes the following case in his book, *Fears and Phobias.* A twenty-year-old woman who was unmarried and worked as a typist had suffered from social phobias for three years before coming for treatment. In the previous year she had not left the house alone except to go to work, and she had stopped working in the last two months.

She was afraid people were looking at her, she feared she would shake while drinking any beverage in public, and she feared all social situations. Generally, this woman was even anxious when at home and had panic attacks there.

Another phobia which Dr. Marks describes in *Fears and Phobias* also shows the extent to which such problems can pervade a person's life. Anthropophobia, or fear of people, includes fear of blushing, a terrible fear of one's eyes meeting the eyes of another person, general uneasiness when in the company of others, and a feeling that one's own looks are ugly. Anthropophobics often bow their heads in the middle of conversations, find it painful to communicate with others, and are generally depressed. Some people who suffer this phobia feel so unattractive that they cannot even talk to their own children comfortably.

Fear of falling in the absence of visual support is one of the less common phobias, but it is an interesting one which shows how crippling a phobia can be. Dr. Marks describes in his book a forty-nine-year-old housewife who was "furniture bound." A year before she came to the hospital for treatment, she'd had a dizzy spell while running for a bus and had had to lean against a lamppost for support. After a number of such attacks, she gradually became unable to walk without holding on to furniture or a wall for support. If she stood more than a foot away from some visible means of support, she became terrified. There was no physical reason for her need to lean on something, and she was quite comfortable when sitting or lying down.

Joe's school phobia is another example of a phobia that can rule a person's life. School phobia is often encountered by experts who work with emotionally disturbed children. Many children have a difficult time with the first few days at school, but they adjust quickly to the separation from home and to the new people they meet at school. Periods of anxiety about school and refusal to attend appear from time to time during many children's school years, but they are usually of short duration. For Joe, the fear of school seemed ever present. It began when he was nine years old and refused to go to school. He gave no explanation at first but later said he was afraid of being hurt by the class bully. He also expressed a fear of fainting during assembly.

When Joe's mother encouraged him to get ready for school in the morning, he complained of headaches and nausea. Sometimes he actually vomited. And the more anxious his mother became about the situation, the more Joe's complaints increased. He could not eat breakfast until his mother reassured him that he would not have to go to school. Then he'd feel better for the rest of the day unless his mother tried to persuade him to go to school in the afternoon. Pressure to get him to go to school intensified his fear responses, and he stayed home for several months at a time.

A phobia such as Joe's is more apt to be brought to the attention of social workers, psychologists, psychiatrists, school counselors, or other mental health workers than one that occurs only occasionally. For example, a fear of horses might not be recognized by anyone but the phobic person because it is not difficult for most people to avoid horses.

A classic example of phobia which is often cited involves horses in the year 1909. At that time, their presence was much more common than it is today. Sigmund Freud reported the case of a five-year-old boy, Hans, who was terrified by horses. According to Freud, who studied the case in great detail mainly through discussions with the father, the boy's fear of being bitten by horses was rooted in his feelings of hostility toward his father and sexual desire toward his mother. Although Freud only saw the boy once, he related the boy's fear to the frightening impulses to attack the father. The boy really feared that his father would find out about his feelings and punish him, but unconsciously changed the fear of father to fear of horses. The outline of the theory, although not completely accepted, forms some of the basis for later theories about the development of phobias.

According to Freud's theory, phobias stem from impulses or urges that one attempts to repress into the unconscious. Consciously, these take the form of fears or anxieties about an unrelated object or situation. In this way, the individual is protected from recognizing the true nature of the situation.

According to this theory, known as psychodynamic theory, the person who has withdrawn from difficult conflicts that lie within himself or herself has focused the fear on an object or a situation which seems entirely unrelated to the original problem. For example, fear of retribution for aggressive thoughts or sexual desires or fear of being left alone may surface as claustrophobia, agoraphobia, etc. Therapists may do a great deal of probing into a person's past before uncovering the basis of the phobic behavior.

Not everyone agrees with this theory. Many therapists and researchers belong to the behaviorist school, which blames phobias on the attachment of an intense fear response to a traumatic experience or to a response learned from a member of the family. In *Behavior Therapy*, Aubrey J. Yates points out that Freud's famous little Hans apparently underwent some traumatic experiences with horses at a very early age. Evidence appears overwhelming that in at least some cases, an early traumatic experience appears to be one of several factors that may influence the development of a phobia.

Another classic study on the origin of phobias is the case known as "little Albert" to generations of psychologists. The famous behaviorist psychologist John B. Watson and a collaborator, Rosalie Rayner, worked with an eleven-month-old child named Albert who was the son of a wet nurse at a children's home in Baltimore, Maryland, in 1920. The researchers were interested in demonstrating that a fear could be produced experimentally, and they performed an experiment on the child which many people who read about it regard as cruel. This seems especially true since the child unexpectedly left the hospital when the fear was still present.

Little Albert, who was reared from birth in a hospital environment because of his mother's employment, appeared to be a stolid and unemotional child. He had never shown signs of fear, and he appeared to enjoy himself when presented with live animals such as a rabbit, a white rat, a dog, and a monkey.

For the experiment, the white rat was presented to Albert. When he reached for it, the experimenter made a loud noise by striking a steel bar behind the boy's head. This startled Albert and caused him to cry. After the fifth repetition of the experience in which the presence of the white rat and the noise were paired, Albert reacted with fear when he saw the rat. Later, the fear was generalized to other furry objects such as a rabbit, a Santa Claus mask, a fur neckpiece, and fluffy material. The demonstration indicated to many psychologists that phobias could be generated by a simple conditioning experience such as the one described. The fear was transferred by association from the loud noise to the rat and then to other furry animals and things which resembled the white rat. This experiment, despite its cruel aspects, has played a part in many of the experimental means of treating phobias. Some of these are described in the next chapter.

Despite the importance of this experiment in later treatment methods, the apparent ease with which little Albert was conditioned to fear has been questioned. While some experiments that followed seemed to support Watson and Rayner's conclusions, other experiments were negative. In one case, a fourteen-month-old girl was tested in her high chair with a painted toy duck in the place of the rabbit. The noise made behind her was extremely loud, but even after fifty attempts she showed no fear response. The experimenter suggested that the girl was not afraid of noise because she had already been deconditioned by her noisy brothers.

A more systematic attempt to reproduce the conditioned fear response was carried out in 1934. Fifteen babies about the age of Albert were studied. Six objects were presented as stimuli, and a bell was used to startle the children. The technique did not appear to produce fear responses, but it, too, was criticized. In this case, it may have been too complicated, while in the case of Albert, the conditioning seemed too quick and easy.

Those who study phobias agree that there is still a great deal to be learned. While most phobias appear to involve more than simple associations between a neutral stimulus and an unpleasant stimulus as in Albert's case, no single theory explains all of the ways fears are learned. Some may be the result of deep-seated childhood problems, as described by Freud, while others may be learned by repeated or traumatic conditioning. It does appear that certain stimuli produce fear reactions much more easily than others.

The case of Peter is famous in the literature on phobias because his is considered the first recorded case of deconditioned fear. Peter suffered from intense fear of animals, possibly brought about by threats from his mother. When Mary Cover Jones, an outstanding therapist, began working with Peter, he was so afraid of small animals that he would scream and fall on his back in his crib at the mere sight of one. He was afraid of fur coats, feathers, and furry things, but he showed no fear of wooden toys or other objects.

In order to help Peter overcome his phobia, he was introduced to play sessions with three other children who had no fear of rabbits. A rabbit was brought into the room during a part of each session. After about nine sessions, the children were given some candy just before the rabbit was introduced. About forty-five play sessions were conducted over a period of about six months, and Peter's progress was tested from time to time by letting him see the rabbit when he was alone. At the end of the experiment he was no longer afraid of the rabbit, but he still had some fear of a feather and a fur coat.

Peter's home life was troubled and, as in the case of Hans, it has been suggested that some of his fear originated in combination with fears of separation from attachment figures. Many children who show intense fear of animals may also have experienced disturbed family situations.

What is the origin of school phobia? Two similar theories are offered here. One is based on the premise that the fear is actually a fear of separation from mother rather than a fear of school. Many children will go to school if their mothers go along, but this in itself does not prove that the phobia is based on fear of separation. As mentioned earlier, all fears tend to be lessened by the presence of a friend or relative. Many school phobias have been shown to be the result of acute anxiety in the child combined with increased anxiety in the mother when the child begins school and makes the break from home ties. Some children fear that their mothers will not be present when they return from school, either because of desertion or death. Some authorities feel that in many cases of school phobia, the fear of school is a substitute fear, or a more palatable fear which replaces that of separation from mother.

On the other hand, since many school phobias don't appear until children have reached the age of eleven or twelve, it has been suggested that the school phobia develops as a result of an unrealistic self-image. A child who has been brought up to expect easy success may fail because of the lack of ability to cope with frustrations. Competition in school can destroy the self-image that an overprotective mother has helped to develop, so returning to her is a way of avoiding the fear response.

School phobia is not the same thing as truancy. Truants skip school without telling their parents, while children with school phobia simply refuse to go to school, remain at home, and exhibit intense fear when pressured into going. School phobias, as well as other phobias, vary in seriousness. Some phobias are not especially troublesome because they are confined to rare situations or objects. Some even disappear without special treatment. Other phobias may cause significant disruption in the life of an individual and may hinder his or her future development. Severe school phobia is an example of a phobia which may cause far-reaching problems if left untreated. There are many cases in which a phobia was found to be only one among a number of symptoms or indications of emotional disturbance. Fortunately, even many severely crippling phobic conditions respond to a variety of treatment methods.

chapter 6

OVERCOMING PHOBIAS

The approaches to dealing with phobias seem almost as numerous as the kinds of phobias themselves. Many phobias are present in people who suffer from other emotional problems, and treatment in such cases is indeed complex. No attempt will be made in this book to describe involved cases. Many times people obtain professional help for phobias with the hope that their depressions or other problems which are difficult to talk about will be treated along with the phobia. And many times they are.

Many simple phobias just disappear as unexplainably as they appeared, as was the case with five-year-old Liz. Even though Liz lived in the city where she had never seen a spider, she developed an intense fear of them. Her knowledge was confined to spiders in story books, but the pictures made them seem very real. Liz imagined there were spiders in her bed at night, even though thorough searching by her parents never produced one. Liz's parents explained to her that spiders are helpful because they eat harmful insects. They explained that spiders avoid contact with people, so unless she bumped into a spider, one would not bite her. Even then, only black widows and rare kinds have harmful bites. While this knowledge did not immediately relieve her fears, Liz gradually learned that spiders would not harm her. As the years passed, the childhood phobia disappeared.

A group of people whose fear of dogs continued into adult life volunteered for a program designed to find a way to overcome their fear. The origin of the individuals' fears varied, but the majority remembered being bitten when they were young and/or being constantly warned by a parent about going near large dogs. One volunteer was comfortable with a family dog but was frightened of all strange dogs even when they were leashed, especially when she encountered them in an elevator. Psychologist Judith Sills tested the volunteers at the New School for Social Research, where she used slides of various dogs as part of the experiment. The volunteers attended sessions one day a week for seven weeks during which time they learned to relax. They rested on rubber mats in a darkened room where slides of dogs were projected on a 10' x 20' wall.

At first, color slides of small friendly dogs were shown. Then dogs that were larger and less friendly appeared on the wall, one by one, while the volunteers continued to relax. The final slide showed a very large dog, leashed but lunging. Anyone who was frightened during the experiments could press a button at his or her side that would flash a light near the projector, and the pictures would be stopped. Some volunteers grew to feel so comfortable with dogs by the end of the program that they could open a door into a room where they knew there would be a dog on a leash, walk in, and in some cases pet the dog.

This procedure, known as systematic desensitization, is a variation of one of the most effective methods of treating phobias. It was developed by Professor Joseph Wolpe of Temple University in the 1950's. Positive reinforcement such as praise for the patient's ability to relax after the feared object or a picture of it is presented helps achieve the goal. In Wolpe's technique the sequence of events follows the pattern of *relax—imagine— relax—stop imagining*. For example, a person who has a phobia about hospitals but must undergo an operation might be instructed to imagine a picture of the outside of a hospital, then asked to stop picturing the hospital and go on relaxing.

After a short time the person might next be told to picture the inside of a hospital, then asked to imagine him or herself in a hospital bed, and finally, after a series of steps, be guided to the operating table by the therapist. The first stimulus is the feared object or situation present verbally in a mild form. The person continues to imagine increasingly fearful situations under the guidance of the therapist so that with each step some of the anxiety is dissipated. Eventually, the person can imagine the most fearful situation without the usual anxiety. When this happens, the transference to the real object usually evokes no fear.

Another process for relieving fears is known as habituation. The participants learn not to respond to a situation when it is not followed by anything of consequence. Learning that something is harmless from direct observation or by experience is very different from merely being told this is true. In some techniques, a person is gradually confronted with the actual fearful situation. For example, consider the case of Tony. Tony was so afraid of water that he wore a life preserver when he took a bath. He was embarrassed to let his family know this and pretended he played a game with the preserver when in the tub. Tony knew it was silly to feel that he could drown in the tub, but he continued to live with his phobia until he heard about another boy at school who was being treated for a fear of closed places. Then he told his parents the truth about his life preserver. They were aware that Tony would never go in the water at the lake, nor would he go in a boat or participate in any other activities near water. But they had not realized the extent of his fear.

Part of Tony's treatment was to imagine that he was taking a bath in a very deep tub of water. Each small detail was described, and Tony was told to imagine that he was slipping under the water. "You are slipping lower and lower into the tub," suggested the psychologist. "Now the water is coming in your mouth and your nose." The first time Tony imagined this situation he was terribly frightened. But the scene was repeated again and again until he learned that the only terrible part of the experience was his own fear. Each time, he was made to imagine the worst thing that could happen; but although he even imagined drowning in the tub, he was never harmed.

During the sessions, the psychologist talked with Tony and discovered the origin of his intense fear through long periods of questioning.

From time to time, he learned small bits of information about Tony's early experiences and about one traumatic experience in which he had wandered off alone and nearly drowned in a shallow stream. Tony recalled that his mother had warned him many times not to go near the stream when he was alone because he might drown. Tony's phobia had existed for so long that he had forgotten about his terrible experience in the stream until he talked with the psychologist. He unlearned his fear of water by first imagining the most threatening situation, such as being immersed in deep water, then gradually becoming accustomed to actually bathing in shallow streams under pleasant and secure conditions.

Professor Thomas G. Stampfl, a psychologist at the University of Wisconsin at Milwaukee, formulated the principles of implosive therapy in which a person is forced to confront intensive fears until they are lessened by familiarity. For example, people who watch gruesome films of traffic accidents as part of their penalty for driving offenses become quite upset by what they see, but the person who runs the projector and watches the film again and again displays little reaction to its horrors. According to Professor Stampfl, implosive therapy encourages patients

to challenge their problems directly. It has been
described as a way of "staring down one's nightmares."

Sometimes a phobia can be extinguished by
having another person demonstrate that the
feared situation or object is not harmful. Take
the strange case of a nineteen-year-old woman.
The object of her phobia was earthworms. Although this did not restrict her life in any great
way, she avoided picnics in the grass and would
not walk in grass or other areas where earthworms might be found. Watching another person handling earthworms to bait a fishhook,
mixing them in the soil of a flowerpot, and
coming to no apparent harm might have lessened her fear.

A variation of the above method actively involves the person with the phobia. After seeing
another person demonstrate the absence of danger in the feared situation, the person is persuaded to participate gradually. Suppose a woman is
afraid of cats and panics whenever she sees one.
Treatment would consist of first having her
watch at a distance as a friend holds a pet cat.
Then she would be persuaded to allow the friend
to bring the cat closer. Gradually she'd be encouraged to tackle the frightening situation of
touching the cat while the owner held it. Then

she'd attempt to stay in a room with the cat walking freely around her. As she became less anxious, she might eventually be able to hold the cat.

The use of another person is most likely to be successful if the model is a therapist trained in helping people to cope with phobias. Suppose a man is afraid of snakes. The therapist would persuade the man to subject himself, step by step, to procedures which range from having the snake in a cage in the same room to touching the snake in the manner in which the therapist does. This process might take many sessions, for the man would not be encouraged to move from one step to another until he could comfortably do so.

Many different approaches, from simple to complex, are used to help people overcome their phobias. The technique known as reinforced practices seems much like common sense. For example, children who are afraid of the dark may be praised for remaining in a dark room for progressively longer periods.

Sometimes combinations of several techniques are used, as happened with a four-year-old boy who had a noise phobia. Loud sounds caused him to panic, and no one could predict whether he would run away from the sound or toward it. When a large noisy truck came down the street he was as likely to run out of the yard in the direction of the truck as he was to run inside and hide. The danger involved in such a phobia is obvious, so it is no wonder that his parents sought help to remove the phobia.

The therapist in this case used a combination of systematic desensitization, muscle relaxation, and counterconditioning. Working with the boy, the therapist made a list of noises in the order of the least frightening to the most frightening. The list ranged from such things as a piece of paper being crumpled, glass breaking, the noise of an airplane, a trash can falling, a board falling to the floor, a heavy piece of steel falling to the floor, the noises of crowds, thunder, a siren, a cannon, and the bursting of a balloon, to the firing of a gun. The therapist began by first teaching the boy how to relax. The boy learned to tighten or tense arm, leg, and other muscles throughout his body and then relax them.

Part of the fear reduction technique involved having the boy imagine he was listening to noises that became increasingly loud. When he became very anxious, he was supposed to signal by raising a finger. The boy never raised a finger while he was imagining the noises. But when the noises were actually presented, he was still frightened. The technique of imagining fearful noises did not seem to be accomplishing anything, so the therapist and the boy's parents cooperated in a program of providing actual noises in controlled situations. In the sessions with the therapist, a louder noise was made in the presence of the boy after he could tolerate soft noises without excessive fear. For example, the therapist would drop a board from a distance of an inch above the floor, then drop one from a distance of several feet. The whole hierarchy of noises on the list were not presented in the therapy sessions, but the boy's parents cooperated in everyday situations. The parents were taught the importance of relaxation and the gradual increase in the loudness of sounds that had formerly frightened the boy. He eventually became so comfortable with loud noises that he could join his father at target practice. At first, he stayed far away from the gun, but later he was able to stand close to his father when the gun was fired.

An interesting kind of counterconditioning was used to help this boy overcome the fear of a balloon popping. Before therapy, just the sight of a balloon frightened him. The father placed a dime inside a partially inflated balloon and the boy had to break it to get the money. He had to produce the noise himself in this case. As his fears were reduced through a brief muscle relaxation procedure, increasingly inflated balloons were popped. The size of the balloons were increased until the boy could break a large, fully inflated balloon without signs of fear. So through a combination of techniques, the phobia of a very young boy was eliminated.

Tranquilizers, sedatives, hypnosis, and psychotherapy are all used to help people overcome phobias. Although some techniques are criticized as just "band-aid" cures which do not get at the roots of the problem, those who are able to master their phobias without developing other undesirable symptoms may well feel that even a "band-aid" method is a good one.

Since every case is different, what helps relieve one person's phobia may not help in another case. Evaluations of the various approaches are still being made. In many cases, long-established phobias have been overcome in a few months and have not recurred in the follow-up periods of many months or even years. This gives encouragement to people who can afford only a short type of treatment.

chapter 7

FEAR OF DEATH AND DYING

Fear of death is universal. Death has always been frightening and mysterious even though it happens to each person. The intensity of the fear ranges widely from a relatively small number of people who suffer from a phobia to those who seldom consider that death can happen to them. Most people, in fact, cannot conceive of their own dying. This is not surprising, since psychiatrists believe that the unconscious mind cannot imagine its own ending except through an accident. Death, quite naturally, is associated with suffering. So the fear of death blends with the fear of suffering. Death is also associated with punishment for a bad act, and this creates feelings of guilt.

The word *death* is avoided even at funerals. Language there is usually couched to avoid a direct reference to death. Dead people are referred to as "loved ones" and "dearly departed" and are "laid to rest" rather than buried. They are shown at viewings with peaceful smiles. Careful cosmetic grooming makes them appear as lifelike as possible. Every effort is made to help the living conceal the fact of death from themselves for as long as possible. Those who do not feel the loss personally need not come to grips with death even at another person's funeral. Overcoming the terror of death can take place only when one sees through the smiling masks of those who surround the dying.

The taboo about death that prevents many people from being comfortable with the subject is lifting somewhat, but widespread education is needed to help large numbers of people attain a mature attitude toward dying. Not many years ago, medical schools avoided the topic of death, and most doctors and nurses working in hospitals concentrated on saving lives with a minimum concern for the feelings of the terminally ill. Since the function of a hospital is to cure, death is considered a failure there. The terminally ill may be targets of great efforts to retain life through medical technology if such life-saving equipment is available even though they are emotionally ready for death.

Fear of death has increased partly because large numbers of people die in hospitals rather than at home. So death has become less familiar to the young and seems less a part of the normal life cycle to everyone. Even those adults who have tried to understand death as a natural part of life find their emotional attitudes have not changed a great deal.

Professor Robert J. Kastenbaum, a psychologist and the editor of *Omega: The Journal of Death and Dying*, cites an experiment of his in which he asked women to interview a man they thought to be a hospital patient. Some of the women were merely told that the man was sick, while others were told that he was terminally ill. The first group reacted more warmly to the man than the group that thought he was dying. The latter seemed to shrink away and avoid eye contact. Professor Kastenbaum reported that even those women who had expressed an open attitude about death in a questionnaire seemed uncomfortable when confronted with a man they thought was dying.

Still, many signs of new attitudes about the frightening subject of death and dying have been evident during the past decade or two. In addition to improvement in many hospital situations, there is a new openness and curiosity about the subject among people in general. Many books about death and dying have been written. In addition to professional journals devoted to the subject, there are numerous articles on death in a wide variety of publications for the general reader as well as professional healers, the clergy, and social workers. Courses and symposiums on death are popular at many age levels. No longer is fear of death a subject reserved for the very old.

Dr. Elisabeth Kübler-Ross, a Swiss psychiatrist practicing in Illinois, has done much to alter attitudes about death and dying. Dr. Kübler-Ross reports that she seldom saw a dead person during her training as a hospital resident. The dead appeared to be almost magically whisked out of sight. Since that time, her work with physicians, nurses, and terminally ill patients has helped alleviate the fear of death for many. Her book, *Death and Dying*, is credited as a motivating force in helping to make the study of death acceptable.

According to Dr. Kübler-Ross, children are not afraid of death, but they learn to fear it because of the actions of people around them. Many adults try to shield children from death because they themselves are so uncomfortable with it. Since our culture teaches us to mask our own fear, anger, grief, and helplessness at the prospect of death, this is not surprising.

Death is not understood as final by children under four years of age. Many young boys and girls help to bury pets and then expect the pets to come alive again the next morning or next season. A young child cannot understand that the separation is permanent when a parent or loved one dies. At about the age of six, children see death as a punishment. A year later they begin to understand that death is permanent but rarely fear it until their ninth year. Of course this is merely a general age pattern and does not apply to all children.

According to Robert Jay Lifton and Eric Olsen in their book *Living and Dying*, the way a child responds to death affects his or her whole personality development. Relaxed conversations with older people who have experienced the loss of friends and relatives can help a child deal with death. For example, a child may develop guilt feelings about the death of someone close if there is no discussion. In some cases, a child may think it is not safe to love because a person close to him or her has died. The child may think that something s/he thought or did caused the death. Open discussion of death and its causes may help to avoid serious conflicts for a child.

Children who are terminally ill often suffer more than necessary because of the way they are treated by adults. According to a study of leukemic children in California by Dr. John J. Spinetta of San Diego State University, parents, doctors, and nurses frequently tend to lessen the amount of contact with a terminally ill child. The child may feel additional anxieties because of this increasing isolation. The adults do not purposely add to the child's problems, but their own fear of death prevents them from dealing comfortably with problems of dying. Medical workers now encourage parents to answer a child's questions about the seriousness of his or her illness honestly. They have found that this minimizes a child's fears about life and death.

Terminally ill children in some hospitals are under the supervision of those trained to deal with death. Children play games in which they take turns being those who bring death and those who take it away. Cops and robbers, playing hospital, and other games help to prepare them for the final event.

Young and old who are terminally ill appear to go through some typical stages before dying. At first, there is shock and disbelief. Even though denial may not be total, the awful and fearful prospect of death is too much to accept at first. Then there is a period of anger, which may be expressed against those who are able to live longer. This is followed by a period of bargaining with God or fate in the hope of gaining more time to do things yet undone. People plead with God for an extra week, or month, or year. This is followed by a stage of depression in which the dying person mourns his or her own death and the loss of the people they love and the things that are meaningful in life. Then there is an acceptance of the oncoming death, a quiet calm, and a willingness to live the remaining days as fully as possible.

The above stages are not the same for all people. They do not last the same length of time, and they can overlap. Some people never reach the end of this developmental process, and some reach it more easily than others. People who have found life gratifying and have many good personal relationships seem less fearful of death than those who have unfinished obligations, overconcern about material wealth, large amounts of material wealth, and/or a phobia about death and dying.

A program at the National Cancer Institute is helping doctors to overcome their own fears of death. Doctors are as fearful of death as are their patients, and in some cases their fears are even greater. By bringing them together in seminars to discuss their own helplessness and rejection in the presence of death and the feelings they have when dealing with terminally ill patients, Dr.

Kenneth L. Artiss, a psychiatrist, and Dr. Arthur S. Levine, a cancer specialist, help doctors come to grips with their own apprehensions about death. These specialists feel that only those doctors who resolve their own fears can lend psychological support to patients who fear death. As a result of understanding help from doctors, nurses, social workers, psychologists, clergy, and families who are educated in the roles they play, fewer people die bitterly.

Since the biological purpose of fear is to secure survival, fear of death is not unnatural. Fear is caused by the threat of loss, and the loss of one's life is indeed total. Fear and anger arise from similar causes: loss, harm, frustration, and threat. In the case of fear, these things are in the future, while in the case of anger, they are usually in the past. When there is knowledge of impending death, the anger comes soon after one learns of it, but the anger is caused by the same prospects of physical harm and threat to survival.

Although fear and anger about death remain with many individuals to the end of their lives, the care of the dying is changing dramatically. There are growing numbers of trained nurses, counselors, and others who help the dying to express their fear and anger. The idea of a specially designed facility for the dying has come from England, where about thirty "hospices" are in operation. These are cheerful, homelike places where families and pets may stay. The first hospice in the United States at New Haven, Connecticut, is modeled after similar facilities in England.

Home care for the dying is also improving, and most dying people prefer to remain at home as long as possible. Hospices emphasize help in home care and offer guidance in drug and emotional therapy. Relatively few people will die in hospices or at homes which benefit from being directly connected with them, but what is learned there may soon be used to help large numbers of people. Certainly, open discussion of death and dying may enable people to fear it less.

chapter 8

ARE YOUR FEARS DIFFERENT?

Are your fears common among people in general, or is there something strange about you because you are afraid of the dark, or of being lonesome, or of flying in an airplane? Fear and alarm are healthy responses to danger, but some of the responses no longer apply to the human animal and seem irrelevant in today's world.

Certain fears which once helped to protect humans are no longer needed, but various experimenters have found some basis for the theory that there is a genetic preparedness which makes certain things more readily feared than others.

In 1929 an experiment in the acquisition of fear and inherited tendencies was performed by an English psychologist, C. S. Valentine, on his own child. The record of this case study is explored in many psychology classes. When Valentine's small daughter was sitting on her mother's lap, he observed the child's reaction to a small pair of opera glasses on a nearby table. Whenever she reached for the glasses, he blew a harsh blast on a whistle. Although she turned to see where the noise had come from, the little girl did not cry with fright. Later in the day, when she was sitting on her father's lap, her brother brought her a woolly caterpillar. Since she had never before been so close to a caterpillar, this was a strange experience. She turned away, then turned back, and as she did, there was a harsh blast on the whistle. This time she screamed in fright.

Valentine reports that the process was repeated four times and that his daughter screamed in terror each time. He felt that the whistle accentuated her attitude toward the caterpillar. The noise produced the slight added shock needed to make the fear of the caterpillar burst forth. This experiment seems to indicate that there was something special about the caterpillar that was not present with the opera glasses. This special something has been referred to as a natural clue, for it has been noted again and again that people tend to fear insects, snakes, and certain other animals. If this is true, was the white rat in the previously described experiments with little Albert really a neutral clue?

As you can see, no one really knows whether or

not a person is born with a built-in readiness to acquire certain fears or whether all fears are learned with the same degree of ease. But according to those who feel that some fear responses are the result of naturally occurring clues, these responses are part of the basic behavioral equipment of humans. The natural clues are those in which there is or once was a threat of danger. They are the ones for which man is biologically prepared, such as loud noises, loss of support, rapid approach of strangers, darkness, large animals, and creatures with slithery motions.

Some of the experiments with chimpanzees and snakes have already been mentioned. The following experiments illustrate another approach to the study of fear of strange objects. Although a four-month-old chimpanzee has no fear of its handler, it shows fear responses to other humans. The strange person is different from the one the young chimp has learned to trust. Even the sight of another chimpanzee who is anesthetized, and therefore motionless, causes intense fear. Psychologist D. O. Hebb reported that young chimpanzees showed fear in the presence of a clay model of a chimpanzee head, and that fear of other parts of the body was spontaneous whether the parts were real or imitation. The novel, strange, or unfamiliar is apt to cause spontaneous fear in many species.

Freud theorized that fears were carried by the "memory of the race," but his followers deplored and deemphasized his interest in "constitutional predisposition" being transmitted through heredity. Carl Jung was convinced that there was a "collective unconscious" and that there was a storing of racial memories in the genes of individuals. To this day, there is disagreement among authorities about whether or not human beings are more ready to learn fears of certain objects or events than others, but as we consider our own fears, it is interesting to note how common many of them are.

Freud recognized the connection between separation and fear early in the twentieth century. He observed that anxiety in children is originally nothing more than an expression of the fact that they are feeling the loss of the person they love. A major theme of John Bowlby's book, *Separation: Anxiety and Anger*, is that fear of separation is often camouflaged. He stresses the importance of the mother or attachment figure in the development of a child's personality. Dr. Bowlby believes that fear of separation in childhood plays a more important part in the development of separation anxieties in adults than many psychiatrists realize. Many parents use the threat of abandonment or separation as a form of discipline, never intending to carry out such a threat.

A parent may threaten to go away if the child does not behave, send the child away, or summon an alarming figure to come and take the child away.

Although fear of separation from a mother or other significant figure cannot really be proved as an innate fear, psychiatrists, psychologists, and others who study personality development attribute many neuroses and character disorders to such fears. Separation can result from isolation or from abandonment, two conditions that are considered natural clues. Dr. Marshall H. Klaus believes that separation of mother and child immediately after birth can have dramatic effects on the mother-child behavior bond and on future behavior. Many professionals have examined the effect of long-term separation, its potential role in a child's personality development, and its contribution to emotional problems in later years.

Fear of darkness is one of the possibly preprogrammed fears that often continues long after childhood. Children are commonly afraid of the dark, perhaps because two natural clues are present when one is alone in the dark: strangeness and isolation. An inky black room is a totally unfamiliar place. Things that are familiar in daylight often take on strange forms at night. A dimly lit basement has shadowy recesses. Bedroom curtains that blow in the wind form strange shadows. There is also a fear of being attacked when one is in the dark, so it is not surprising that this fear is so common.

Most parents attempt to help their children overcome the fear of the dark in many ways. Some parents, however, are unusually cruel and use the child's fear to obtain good or desired behavior. A parent may threaten to lock a child in a dark room or closet if s/he does not behave, and for some children, this threat becomes a reality. Fortunately, most parents help their children overcome the fear of the dark by reassuring them that they are nearby, thus eliminating one natural clue (that of being alone) and making the darkness far less frightening.

Three psychologists, Frederick H. Kanfer, Paul Karoly, and Alexander Newman, experimented with forty-five kindergarten children in a large midwestern city in the United States. They wanted to find out if they could reduce fear of darkness more effectively through the popular psychological technique known as systematic desensitization if they combined it with verbal clues. The children were chosen carefully. All were so afraid of the dark that they would not remain alone in a dark room for more than a very brief time. The average time at the beginning of the experiment was twenty-seven seconds.

The experiment was carried out in a darkened schoolroom, which was familiar to the children. It was conducted in a scientific manner, with some children acting as a control group (one which was given neutral information). Each child was in contact with an experimenter by electronic equipment, and each could illuminate the room at will. The experimental group was divided in two. One, known as the competence group, used the verbal clue: "I am a brave boy. I can take care of myself in the dark." The other, called the stimulus group, was taught to verbalize as follows: "The dark is a fun place to be. There are many good things in the dark." The control group used "Mary had a little lamb. Its fleece was white as snow."

The experimenters were careful not to frighten the children, and they worked with a complicated procedure. They obtained the best results with children in the competence group and observed, "Emphasis on the child's competence to deal with the stress-inducing experience of exposure to the dark resulted in the longest tolerance times."* The neutral and stimulus groups did not

*Journal of Consulting and Clinical Psychology, 1975, vol.43, no.2, pp. 251–8.

differ from each other in ability to stay alone in the dark.

While this experiment was complex and involved many more factors than can be explained here, it does illustrate one way in which fear of darkness can be handled. Just the simple assurance that parents, or someone they know, will come when called is enough to make the dark less frightening for many children. And this fear, as with many other fears of children, does tend to disappear. However, even adults who suffer from a fear of the darkness can be sure that their fear is shared by a large number of people.

Another common fear is that of flying in an airplane. This varies in degree from mild apprehension to the phobic reaction. Since most people do not have to fly in planes, however, it is one of those fears that can often be avoided. However, executives and others who must fly for business reasons are among the many people who have consulted professional therapists for help in overcoming their intense fears. These people are far more apprehensive about flying than about any other kind of trip. No one can convince them by statistics or other practical information that a plane trip is relatively safer than an automobile trip. When they read about a plane accident, they use this information to justify their fear. Reading about the number of people killed on highways each year, however, has little or no affect on the amount of driving these people do. While a phobia is not something that can easily be overcome without the help of a professional, it is comforting to the many people who have some fear of flying to know that theirs is not an uncommon fear.

There are some people who will travel by plane but suffer some mild degree of fear about flight. A survey to explore fear of flying was conducted at an airport under the auspices of Jerome Zimmerman of the School of Social Work, Tulane University. Researchers questioning a number of passengers before and after flights found that people were more likely to admit their fears about flying just after they had left a plane than before boarding one. The researchers believed this might be due to the fact that people who are about to do something which they consider dangerous deny their fear to themselves as well as to others. While fears of flying are somewhat irrational, few who fly have reached the phobic stage. In most cases, fears disappear when people fly frequently.

Fear of public speaking is another fear that is sometimes overcome by experience. From childhood days to old age, many people suffer at the

very thought of speaking in front of a group
even though they may be well qualified to do so.
Standing up alone makes them feel uncomfortable, while speaking as part of a group is less apt to
cause fear. Perhaps this is related to the fear of
isolation and the desire to be close to an attachment figure. Consider a three-year-old girl who
is frightened by the dark and clutches her teddy
bear. Two children walk past a haunted house
holding hands. Two adults are frightened by a
noise while camping out, so they move their
sleeping bags closer together. An earthquake
causes damage in a village, and the people draw
closer together both physically and emotionally.

Although most people reach out to their
friends and relatives in time of danger, there are
people who are afraid to make friends. The
attachment to mother is normally formed without conscious effort, and for most people, both
young and old, the same is true in forming
friendships. But there are many people who are
so conscious of their supposed shortcomings that
they are afraid to risk rejection by their peers.
This is especially true during adolescence, but it
carries over into the lives of some adults.

Fear of not being accepted is a common fear
that allows peer groups to set such standards as
the "right thing to wear" and the "right thing to

say and do." As young people grow away from parents and reach out toward the larger world, fears of not being popular, of not having the money to keep up with the group, of being laughed at, of not being liked by the opposite sex, and of being lonely are very common, private fears. A lonely person feels frighteningly unarmed and unprotected. In *Loneliness: The Fear of Love,** Ira J. Tanner writes about lonely, frightened people. "Fear of love," he states, "is the root cause of every attitude and form of behavior that separates us from each other."

Everyone feels lonely at some times, and this is natural. But loneliness has been called the most common disease of modern times. Many people who suffer from more than an occasional bout of it are now willing to admit this. Perhaps they suffered silently in the past.

In some ways, youthful loneliness appears to be replacing the youthful rebelliousness of the past decades, and it may be one of the leading problems for young people today. New mobility and modern technology have provided a certain amount of freedom; but at the same time, they have given rise to more loneliness and isolation, even in the crowded cities. Family and friendship

*Tanner, Ira J. *Loneliness: The Fear of Love*, New York: Harper and Row, 1973.

bonds are severed more frequently, and loneliness sometimes results from situations beyond one's control. Such conditions produce fear for those who cannot easily reach out for new friends. Those who experience the fear of love, even though they do not recognize this fear, are the people who feel alone in a crowd. They may not even be able to relate comfortably to their own immediate families. Some people have a fear of experiencing good feelings, and this may be related to a fear that they are not lovable.

The fact that loneliness is a form of separation seems obvious, but the degree to which most people fear separation is not. Life begins with separation at birth, and it is here that some professionals believe chronic fear, or anxiety, begins. A baby enters a world that is very different from the secure one it has known in the mother's uterus. Otto Rank, a leading psychoanalyst, presented the theory that birth is such a frightening experience that a person never completely outgrows the fears it creates. Other authorities say that birth is the first experience to activate the innate potential for imagining the final separation from the world, or death. When a baby is born, it is vulnerable to pain and disintegration.

Robert Jay Lifton and Eric Olson, in *Living and*

Dying, suggest that as a person passes through various stages of life, each new step, or "birth," brings with it new death anxieties that are associated with the inborn imagery of separation, existence, and disintegration. The responses of young children to separation from their mothers has already been mentioned in connection with children's fears. Again and again, one finds that when fear is present, a child or adult seeks comfort in the nearness of a familiar person or place.

Even though the number 13 is familiar, many people are superstitious about living on the thirteenth floor of a building. This fear is so prevalent that in many tall buildings the number 13 is skipped when numbering floors because people dislike the "risk" of living or working on the thirteenth floor. Some people avoid going out to shop on the thirteenth day of the month, especially if that date falls on a Friday. Numerous incidents through the years may have appeared to support the idea that such a day is unlucky. Then there is the fact that the thirteenth Tarot card is the card of death. Nevertheless, there are many good things connected with the number 13, too, including the original number of stars and stripes in the American flag. Many superstitions that evoke fear in people are irrational, but almost everyone has his or her own rituals. Even many of the people who say they would *not* be afraid to live on the thirteenth floor of a building would probably avoid doing so, saying "Why take a chance?" Perhaps this, too, is a fear of the unfamiliar.

Superstition is often a "fun" fear. Playing games with fear is common and serves a special purpose. The masks at Halloween are more for fun than fear, but there is an element of fear involved. Originally, Halloween was All Hallows, or All Saints' Day, and was devoted to the dead who were blessed and in heaven. It was a day of devotion to the memory of the dead even in pre-Christian times, but in America today much of the original meaning has been forgotten. Many symbols of death, such as skeletons, skulls, cross-bones, witches, devils, and ghosts, are still part of the holiday scene, however. With the obligations to remember ancient ancestors forgotten, one might consider the child-ghosts as ancestral ghosts returning from the dead to frighten the adults who have neglected their memories. Child-ghosts are appeased with candy and small change, which unconsciously represent sacrifices once offered on the graves of the dead. Ancient burial myths sometimes included a small payment for fare over the Styx, a river in the underworld across which the souls of the dead were ferried. Dr. Martin Grotjahn, in *Beyond Laughter*, suggests that the pumpkin head with lighted candle may represent the funeral bier with the head of the slain enemy as a trophy. He also points out that parents symbolically repeat the ancient sacrifice of children by allowing them to represent the dead in their Halloween costumes, although this act remains in the unconscious.

Many people delight in horror stories and movies, frightening fairy tales, masks, haunted houses, and spooky graveyards. Much the same is true of scary rides in amusement parks. Psychologists suggest that people who find fun in being frightened like a self-chosen dare. They expose themselves to these experiences to prove to themselves that they will not really be hurt by them. It is fun to know that one can deal with such terror. Perhaps it is part of wanting to feel a conquest over fear. Automobile racers, stuntmen like Evel Knievel, test pilots, mountain climbers, and others who put themselves in high-risk situations want to show others, and probably themselves, that they are not afraid.

Suppose you go through a haunted house at an amusement park. You enter the house expecting something scary to happen. The hallway is dark, and spider webs are hanging all around. Of course, you know they are not real and you know that whatever makes you jump will not really hurt you. Still, you enjoy the fun of feeling frightened while knowing there is no real harm.

Bruno Bettelheim describes the use of fear in fairy tales in his book, *The Uses of Enchantment.* This famous psychologist describes the child's unconscious as a battleground full of terrifying fears, death wishes, and hatreds. The violence in fairy tales helps to allay the child's fears by showing that s/he is not the only one who imagines such awful happenings. While fairy tales may frighten a child for a short period of time, Dr. Bettelheim observes that their happy endings dispel anxiety.

Fear is certainly a subject upon which there is much disagreement, whether one is considering its origins or the part it plays in the lives of children and adults. But few disagree that it plays a large part, both constructive and destructive, and that recognizing fear for what it is may be an important step in helping to deal with it positively.

chapter 9

THE MANY FACES OF FEAR

From anxiety that is mild to panic such as that experienced by passengers in a hijacked airplane, fear wears many faces. Anxiety is so universal that it has been considered the second most universal experience (loneliness is the first). Everyone, at some time or another, experiences vague feelings of impending disaster without quite knowing the cause of the threat.

While most people are only mildly anxious, this form of fear varies in intensity and frequency. In some lives, anxiety is always present as a condition that is sometimes referred to as free-floating. While the cause of anxiety may be hidden, sometimes it is clearly linked to some specific event in a person's life. An impending graduation, a job change, a first sexual experience, and a death in the family are just a few examples of events that precipitate increased anxiety.

Individuals differ in their ability to tolerate

anxiety. A situation that evokes a great deal of anxiety in one person may be considered an exciting challenge by another. Consider the cases of Karen and Becky. Karen enjoys making speeches in front of large groups even though she is apprehensive before she steps on the platform. Her body responds to this fear in many ways. Her brain alerts certain glands in her body to secrete hormones to prepare her for vigorous exertion even though Karen is well aware that there will not be any physical action or unusual strain on her body. Still, the pupils of her eyes dilate, her hearing becomes sharper, her lungs take in more oxygen to fuel the muscles that could be needed for fight or flight. Even the ability of her blood to clot is increased to protect against the excessive bleeding that might occur in a fight. It is the kind of reaction that takes place in everyone, and it has been happening to frightened people ever since the days when fright meant fight or flee. Once Karen reaches the platform and begins to speak, however, she relaxes. Her audience reacts favorably, and she begins to enjoy the situation. All of the physical responses return to the normal state as her fear disappears.

Becky, on the other hand, finds speech-making extremely unpleasant. She dreads the event for days, and when the actual time arrives, she experiences the typical fear reaction. Even as she talks to her audience, the fear remains. And her body continues to respond with a certain amount of fear even after the speech has ended. She begins to dread the day when she will have to speak in public again. So Becky's body continues to be prepared for fight or flight, even though there is no physical danger. She lives in a state of chronic anxiety.

Gina lives in a world of fear where physical danger is a real threat. Her home is in a large city which has a high crime rate. Many of her friends have been mugged both on the street and in their apartments. When Gina goes to the store, her fear is especially great. She clutches her purse and walks rather fast, unconsciously giving clues to potential muggers that she has money and is afraid of losing it. Day and night, Gina consciously or unconsciously experiences fear reactions, as she's waiting for "her turn to come." Even when she is preparing meals, reading, watching television, or listening to music, her body is reacting to her fear because of its built-in automatic defenses against danger. But this kind of nonspecific anxiety cannot be solved by fight or flight, and it continues to affect her body in a way that may cause ill health.

Gina's fear is a result of physical threat. Carl also lives in a world of constant fear, but he is in no physical danger. As an air traffic controller, he experiences many anxious moments as he directs planes in and out of airports. Carl is well aware that one mistake may cost the lives of many people. While he acts with calm attention, his body is always prepared for emergency action. Such a constant state of anxiety often takes its toll in physical changes such as ulcers and other forms of digestive ailments, heart disease, and a wide variety of illnesses. While the fear experienced by air traffic controllers is based on actual danger, the same bodily changes are often suffered by people whose fears are largely imaginary. Since their bodies cannot determine whether or not the danger is real, stress-related diseases can result from fears that have little basis in fact.

The dread of nameless dangers and chronic apprehension may cause an anxiety reaction. This condition is marked by extreme tension. Although the individual feels a definite threat of harm, s/he is unable to find a cause for it or to determine what the danger might be. Symptoms may include the inability to sleep, disturbed sexual and digestive functioning, increased perspiring, rapid pulse, and heart palpitations. The individual who suffers from an anxiety reaction has been compared with the hero in *The Trial*, a novel by Franz Kafka. Here, a man is confronted with a trial but never learns the nature of the charges which are brought against him.

Psychiatrists, psychologists, social workers, and others who work with people suffering from anxiety reactions recognize several types of situations which act as cues for anxiety attacks. For example, something in the environment that brings back memories of a traumatic experience may act as a stimulus. Arousal of unconscious guilt feelings may be another cue.

Suppose Jim is a boy with strong homosexual tendencies of which he is not aware. He spends an evening with a group of people who make fun of homosexuals. Each time the topic of sex is discussed, Jim feels more tense. Although Jim had felt tense and fatigued for several months, he never connected his feelings with anything sexual. Tonight he has some sudden heart palpitations, his breathing becomes more rapid, his palms sweat, and his hands fidget. As the evening progresses, Jim feels a desire to run from the room to get more air.

Following several attacks of this intensity, Jim is encouraged to obtain professional help. After a long period of treatment, he is able to reorient his thought processes and improve his emotional life so that his chronic anxiety is greatly de-creased. When the previously repressed internal conflicts are resolved, he no longer suffers the anxiety attacks.

Many people experience free-floating anxiety that is less intense than Jim's. Some are adults who were severely criticized by parents or were held to extremely high standards when they were children. As adults they are overly concerned about making mistakes and suffer from feelings of guilt if they fail to measure up to the standards set by their parents or themselves.

Very strict obedience to authority is a common mask of fear among adults whose parents treated them severely as children. Others mask their fear with aggression, even as children. The well-known bully acts out of fear. Richard is a big boy, but he is afraid of other children because he feels that no one really cares about him. He very much wants to receive some special attention, but the only way he knows how to get it is by beating up a small boy in his class. When he does, Richard is punished by the teacher. This kind of attention seems better than no attention at all, so despite the unpleasant punishment, Richard continues to repeat his aggressive behavior. He taunts and teases and acts as if he feels important, when all the time he is really afraid that no one likes him.

Fear and the impulse to destroy, or anger,

seem to go hand in hand. Each is caused by many of the same or similar things, such as danger to one's body or possessions, threat to survival, loss, and/or frustration. Fear of scarcity is one of the causes of aggression both in the case of members of small groups such as families, and members of large groups, such as nations. Suppose a nation fears a food shortage, while a neighboring country has a large supply of food. Or suppose one has a shortage of land or other resources, while a nearby country has plenty. Such conditions often play a part in starting wars.

The pressure of fear, either real or imagined, was a major factor in the formation of the Nazi party in Germany before World War II. People banded together when they felt economic, political, cultural, and religious insecurity. They chose authority with security rather than freedom with fear. Hitler gradually took over by playing on that fear. Consider the following words from a Nazi anthem:

Holy Fatherland in danger, thy sons gather round thee,
Encircled by danger,
Holy Fatherland, we all stand together, hand in hand.

The fear-born solidarity of old neighbors against new is common in country villages as well as in sections of large cities. This is especially true when a different ethnic group is being introduced. Fear plays an important role in the development of street gangs where people of the same culture band together. For example, in a section of a large city which was predominately Italian or Irish, adults expressed fears that the blacks were taking over their neighborhood. Children heard their parents talking this way and joined together in gangs to protect their own territory. Together, they felt secure. Their loyalty extended to all members of their own group, and if one was attacked, the whole gang felt obligated to retaliate. Gangs themselves exert power through the fear that they inspire.

Some people seek power over others to mask their own fears. Just as the gang uses solidarity to overcome fear, an individual may use domination. People who are unable to rely on others, people who feel that they are not loved or wanted, and people who are afraid of genuine feeling because they fear their emotions might get out of control often disguise their fears this way. Fear-motivated power is linked with lack of compassion, and the people who wield this kind of power are usually overly concerned with being more successful than others. They compete to attain something that will be desired or envied by others.

Suppose Kim has managed to place herself in a

position of power in a school drama club. She deals with a girl who threatens her by giving the girl a smaller part in a play. This gives Kim a sense of power which she uses to cover her own fears. Kim typically vents her rage on weaker people because she lacks confidence and fears being put down.

There are many other methods people use to disguise their fears. Do you know someone in whom fear is masked as goodness? This is likely to be a person who is extremely critical of others, who is very conscious of taboos, and who tries to instill guilt in others. For example, Tim is very proud of the things he avoids. He does not drink, smoke, keep late hours, or waste time. He is much more concerned with what he does *not* do than with what he does, and he is quick to criticize those who indulge in the things he avoids. Tim tends to run other people's lives "for their own good," but he does very little real living on his own because he is afraid to take a risk. In many ways, Tim is especially critical of the very things he himself would like—but fears—to do.

Sally is the victim of another kind of fear in disguise. Her mother supplies all her needs, but at the same time she seldom gives Sally a chance to think for herself. Even though Sally is in high school, her mother tells her what to eat, what to wear, and how to act. The mother treats the daughter more like a possession than a person. Sally's mother wants to be needed, so she tries to prevent her daughter from becoming independent. The mother masks fear in the name of love and is unconsciously using Sally in her own search for security.

Terror is one of the many faces of fear which makes people act in unusual ways. Terror is an extreme reaction of fear experienced when one is confronted with real danger and can find no way to escape. A child trapped in a burning building, a man confronted by a mugger's gun, a woman whose home is washing away in flood waters are all experiencing terror. Perhaps you have experienced terror when walking on an icy road. You may have been "frozen with fear" as a car skidded toward you and you could not move out of its path.

Terror which stalks those in a hijacked airplane may last for a long period of time. Some of these victims appear to suffer what has been called the hijacker syndrome. Rather than being angry with the terrorists who have put them through the ordeal, they recall the experience with some praise for their captors. Psychologists believe that the hijackers elicit admiration through sheer menace. They hold the lives of the passengers in their hands, and the passengers feel grateful because they have not been killed.

Although victims of a hijacked plane generally experience terror, they can be encouraged to avoid panic. Panic has many definitions, but most include an element of irrational behavior and a certain amount of contagion. Consider the reaction of a group of people in a peacetime disaster such as a large explosion, flood, fire, tornado, or earthquake. The notion that people generally panic in the presence of danger has not been borne out by research. However, panic does arise when certain individuals act for their own advantage and interfere with the orderly activities of others. Suppose a theater is on fire and people have begun to walk in orderly lines toward the exits. Suddenly a few people begin to push. The whole group stampedes in panic toward the exits, clogging them so that no one escapes.

Panic resulted in collective suicide at the famous Cocoanut Grove fire in Boston. This happened one Saturday evening in November of 1942. About a thousand people were crowded into the Cocoanut Grove Night Club, where decorations included poles topped with paper palm leaves and walls hung with cloth. A busboy attempting to replace a light bulb in the ceiling lit a match in order to see better. A paper palm frond caught fire, and from there a flame raced through the decorations. At the cry of *"Fire!"* and the sight of the flames, a singer led ten people to safety in a basement refrigerator room. But most of the others were caught in the panic. Screams grew louder, and people rushed toward possible exits. Some made their way to safety by getting to the roof of the building and leaping to the tops of parked cars below. Others were rushing toward a door when one woman fell down. Bodies began piling up on top of her. Many people were jammed together in a revolving door, where they lost their sense of reason and were caught in a clawing and screaming panic which prevented the door from turning. Fire fighters found other doorways clogged with bodies, which they had to remove before they could get inside to fight the fire. Almost five hundred people died in this fire because panic prevented them from escaping.

More recently, flames trapped many people in the Crefisul Investment Bank Building in São Paulo, Brazil. Here, too, as in other disasters, many people lost their lives as a result of panic. Some victims jumped to death despite cries from the crowds around the building urging them to wait for help. But as the fire raged out of control, frantic people made ropes from curtains and tried to lower themselves to safety even though the makeshift ladders reached just halfway down the building. Two panicked and jumped into ladders, injuring people who were being rescued. One man, a floor supervisor, reported that he hit several workers in the face in an effort to reduce their panic and prevent them from jumping off the hot roof.

Panic broke out during the fire which destroyed the Beverly Hills Supper Club near Cincinnati, Ohio, during Memorial Day Weekend, 1977. Here, between six and seven hundred people were being entertained when a small fire began in the wall of a private dining room. Employees who noticed the fire tried to put it out, while a bus boy stepped to the microphone in the main room and announced that there was a small fire. He asked everyone to stay calm and to leave the building.

For a brief period of time a small number of people filed out, but the rest stayed at their tables and continued to watch the entertainment. Suddenly, the whole building seemed to be engulfed in flames and black smoke. People panicked. Some jumped over the bar while others stampeded toward the exit signs. Exit doorways led through hallways where many people were overcome by smoke as they tried to escape. Bodies fell to the floor and some of the men and women were trampled to death. A few died from the smoke while still at their tables.

The fact that most rooms in the nightclub did not have doors which opened directly to the outside added to the panic. Corridors filled with frightened people became a deathtrap. While there were not as many casualties in this fire as in the one at Cocoanut Grove, it was one of the worst in recent history. Proper fire exits, a sprinkler system, and an earlier call for help may have prevented the Beverly Hills fire from spreading, but the panic added to the number of casualties.

Less than a month after this fire was reported in the newspapers, another nightclub blaze was described in the *New York Times*. On June 9, 1977, a fire killed 41 people in a nightclub in Abidjan, the Ivory Coast capital. Here, too, flames and thick black smoke caused panic among the patrons and some were trampled to death as they rushed toward the exit. Unfortunately, there are many reports of fires in which the fear of panic is involved.

The word *panic* is derived from the "contagious fear" caused by the mythical Greek god, Pan. It is said that Pan was banished to the mountains where he amused himself by giving the lonely traveler sudden frights. Or, according to another version, when Pan took his divine naps in the woods and mortals disturbed his sleep, he chased them, putting his frightening appearance and all the elements that were in his service to use.

Whether or not panic needs to involve contagion is not clear from the above stories of the origin of the word, but a study of the subject by R. Brown, author of *Social Psychology*, indicates that most writers describe panic in terms of some contagion. People may be more apt to panic when they are part of a group. In the case of the famous Orson Welles broadcast of 1938 which announced an attack on Earth by monstrous inhabitants from Mars, people rushed into the streets in panic believing the drama was an actual news release. The group aspect here has been explained as a union of people bound together by the common act of listening to the radio, although some of the contagion may have spread in the streets. Certainly, there is little question that something as dramatic as an invasion from outer space could cause panic.

A broadcast that was based on the Welles program also created panic in Quito, Ecuador, years after the original was heard in the United States. At the time, the people of that country were suffering from chronic political unrest and were in a state of latent fear. The realistic radio reports of an invasion from Mars caused a panic which led to some destruction of a newspaper building. Even after people learned that the broadcast was not based on fact, they continued their angry rampage. This may have been due to the fact that the physical changes which occur during panic were still working.

There is a very different form of panic, which may also end in tragedy. Dr. Joost A. Meerloo writes about "silent panic" during wartime in his book, *Patterns of Panic.** He describes the following conditions in a London shelter during the bombings of World War II: A bomb exploded near the overcrowded shelter, and the electric power system failed. Someone stumbled up the stairs, but there was no screaming or crying to be heard. Everyone was quiet in what Meerloo describes as a sudden upheaval of fear in the pitch dark. When first aid arrived to help the victims, nearly two hundred of the six hundred people were found dead. Postmortems revealed no significant anatomical changes. Had they died of fright?

Death due to panic is described by many tribal doctors. In these cases, panic is due to lack of knowledge and/or complete faith in the power of

*Meerloo, Joost A. *Patterns of Panic*, Westport, Conn.: Greenwood Press, 1950, p. 37.

destruction because of learned taboos. Whether or not individual deaths caused by the curse placed on persons who believe in its power can be classed as panic or some other kind of fright is a matter of definition.

Many cases of death from fright have been reported over hundreds of years. The cases of hysteria resulting from fear of a witch's power are even more numerous. One interesting case in which the fear of a witch's curse was removed involved the use of a chemical known as methylene blue. A Hawaiian physician, Dr. Harold M. Johnson, reported curing severe skin lesions in patients who believed they'd been bewitched. He gave them tablets of methylene blue which turned their urine blue. This action was so impressive that the patients believed the tablets were a countercharm; their fears disappeared, and the skin lesions healed. Hypnosis is a more common way of removing the fear resulting from the curse of a sorcerer.

Whether severe fear reactions are caused by belief in magic or by actual physical reactions, panic is a common response. Once panic begins, it spreads in what seems to be a chain reaction. Unless one can be stopped in the very beginning, even the people who try to stop the panic are likely to be drawn into the same emotional state.

A responsible leader may be able to stop a panicky herd of people but only if s/he is alert enough to act at once.

Preventing panic in times of crisis, whether it be tornado, hurricane, flood, earthquake, explosion, or bombing, is best accomplished by removing the mysterious. When people are prepared for events and know how to act, their fears can be acknowledged and put to work to help prevent harm. Fire drills, flood warnings, and hurricane alerts help both physically and psychologically.

In some areas where earthquakes occur fairly often, efforts are being made to prevent panic at the time of a serious tremor. In Japan, for example, where large masses of earth shift with unusually high frequency, there are definite programs to help deal with a quake's destruction. Noticeable tremors are reported in Japan as often as every ten days. Minor tremors beneath the sprawling plain that supports Tokyo or tremors in the sea around it are observed daily by scientists, but no one knows when the next major earthquake will strike.

Evacuation drills are held in some parts of Japan, and shelters with food and water are available in certain areas. The feelings of preparedness these engender appear to have a calming effect on the people. Children in schools have contests for the best slogans to guide anyone caught in an earthquake. Over a hundred Tokyo roads are officially designated as routes to open areas. These are lined with thousands of fire extinguishers in display cases and hundreds of underground cisterns and emergency pumps. Leaders have been trained to prepare people to take charge of the situation, prevent panic, and help the victims when an earthquake occurs. Hopefully, they can reduce the level of fear to one that helps rather than harms.

While there is still much to be learned about fears and phobias, it is good to know that many masks of fear can be removed and abnormal fears can be conquered. In spite of all the problems which fear causes, one would not want to do away with the fears which warn of danger. The true hero learns to recognize fear, respect it, and on some occasions to laugh at his or her own fears.

For the adventurous, fear has become a green or amber light rather than a red one, a feeling to pursue with caution. Only certain kinds of fear can be enjoyed; others can be tamed by warning systems and crisis counseling. And the little fears that nag at us day by day can be exposed for what they are and brought under control, if not completely removed.

SUGGESTIONS FOR FURTHUR READING

Aronson, Marvin L. *How to Overcome Your Fear of Flying*
New York: Hawthorn Books, Inc., 1971.

Bettelheim, Bruno. *The Uses of Enchantment: The Meaning and Importance of Fairy Tales.* New York: Alfred A. Knopf, 1976.

Bowlby, John. *Attachment and Loss,* Vol. 2 *Separation: Anxiety and Anger.* New York: Basic Books, 1973.

Fox, M. W. *Abnormal Behavior in Animals.* Philadelphia: W. B. Saunders Company, 1968.

Grosser, George, Henry Wechsler, and Milton Greenblatt. *The Threat of Impending Disaster.* Cambridge, Mass.: MIT Press, 1965.

Grotjahn, Martin. *Beyond Laughter: Humor and the Subconscious.* New York: McGraw-Hill, 1966.

Hyde, Margaret O., and Elizabeth Forsyth. *Know Your Feelings.* New York: Franklin Watts, 1975.

Izard, Carrol E. *Patterns of Emotions: A New Analysis of Anxiety and Depression.* New York: Academic Press, 1972.

Joseph, Stephen M. *Children in Fear.* New York: Holt, Rinehart and Winston, 1974.

Kübler-Ross, Elisabeth. *On Death and Dying.* New York: Macmillan, 1969.

Lifton, Robert Jay, and Eric Olson. *Living and Dying.* New York: Praeger Publishers, 1974.

Marks, Isaac H. *Fears and Phobias.* New York: Academic Press, 1969.

Meerloo, Joost A. M. *Patterns of Panic.* Westport, Conn.: Greenwood Press, 1950.

Perkes, Dan. *Eyewitness to Disaster.* Maplewood, N. J.: Hammond, 1976.

Rachman, Stanley. *The Meanings of Fear,* Baltimore: Penguin Books, 1974.

Rachman, Stanley. *Phobias: Their Nature and Control.* Springfield, Ill: Charles C. Thomas, 1968.

Siegal, Mordecai, and Matthew Margolis. *Good Dog, Bad Dog.* New York: Holt, Rinehart and Winston, 1973.

Stein, Maurice, R., Arthur J. Vidich, and David Manning White, eds. *Identity and Anxiety: Survival of the Person in Mass Society.* Glencoe, Ill.: The Free Press of Glencoe, 1969.

Tanner, Ira J. *Loneliness: The Fear of Love.* New York: Harper and Row, 1973.

Wood, John T. *What Are You Afraid Of?* Englewood Cliffs, N. J.: Prentice-Hall, 1976.

Yates, Aubrey, J. *Behavior Therapy.* New York: John Wiley and Sons, 1970.

INDEX

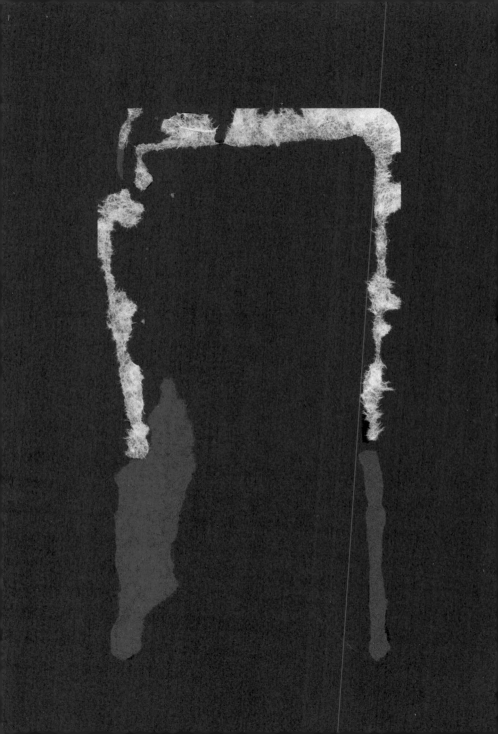